How to Draw a UNICORN

For Kids Ages 4-8

By
Unicorn Publishing

How to Draw a UNICORN

10 DRAWINGS

UNICORN 1

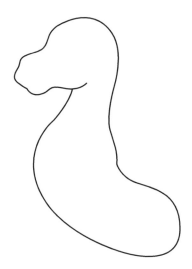

1

Draw the shape of the Unicorn.

2

Draw lines for the Unicorn's legs.

UNICORN 1

3

Draw eyes, eyebrows, nose, ear and lips and lines for chest, belly and unicorn hoof.

4

Draw Unicorn's hair and tail with details.

UNICORN 1

⑤

**Draw the Horn
of the Unicorn.**

⑥

**Finally, delete all
unnecessary lines
to merge the body.**

UNICORN 2

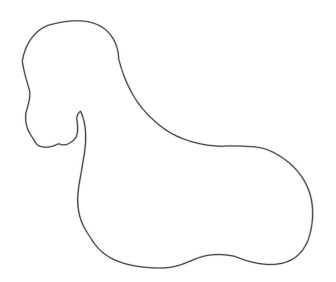

1
Draw the shape of the Unicorn.

2
Draw eyes, eyebrows, nose, ear and lips.

UNICORN 2

③

Draw Unicon's legs and lines for the chin.

④

Draw Unicorn's hair and tail with details.

UNICORN 2

5 Draw the Horn and fur on the legs.

6 Finally, delete all unnecessary lines to merge the body.

UNICORN 3

1

Draw the shape of
the Unicorn.

2

Draw Unicon's legs.

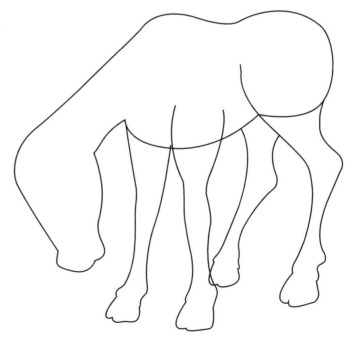

UNICORN 3

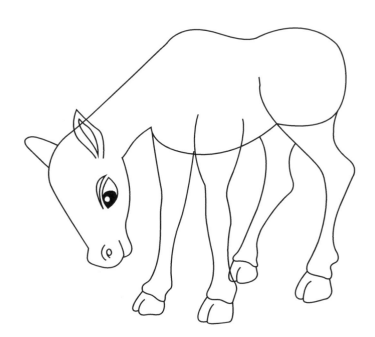

3

Draw eyes, eyebrows, nose, ear and lips and the chin.

4

Draw Unicorn's hair and tail with details.

UNICORN 3

5

Draw the Horn
of the Unicorn.

6

Finally, delete all
unnecessary lines
to merge the body.

UNICORN 3

1
Draw the shape of the Unicorn.

2
Draw Unicon's legs.

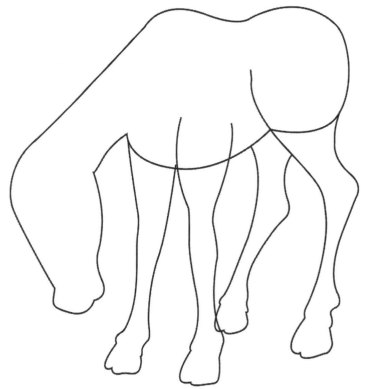

UNICORN 3

3

Draw eyes, eyebrows, nose, ear and lips and the chin.

4

Draw Unicorn's hair and tail with details.

UNICORN 3

5 Draw the Horn of the Unicorn.

6 Finally, delete all unnecessary lines to merge the body.

UNICORN 4

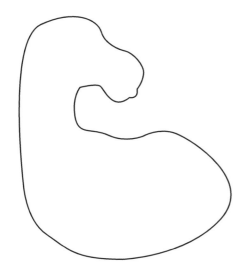

1

Draw the shape of the Unicorn.

2

Draw Unicon's legs.

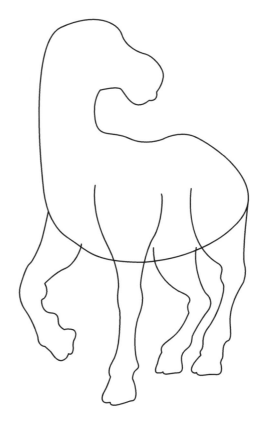

UNICORN 4

 3

Draw eyes, eyebrows, nose, ear and lips and lines for the chin.

4

Draw Unicorn's hair and tail with details.

UNICORN 4

5 Draw the Horn and fur on the legs.

6 Finally, delete all unnecessary lines to merge the body.

UNICORN 5

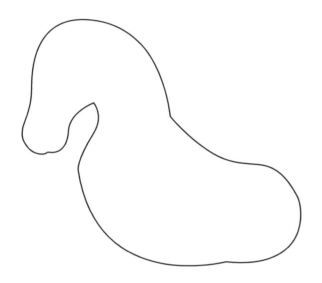

1

Draw the shape of
the Unicorn.

2

Draw Unicon's legs.

UNICORN 5

3

Draw eyes, eyebrows, nose, ear and lips and lines for the neck.

4

Draw Unicorn's hair and tail with details.

UNICORN 5

5 Draw the Horn
and fur
on the legs.

6 Finally, delete all
unnecessary lines
to merge the body.

UNICORN 7

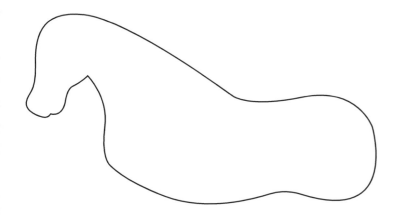

1

Draw the shape of the Unicorn.

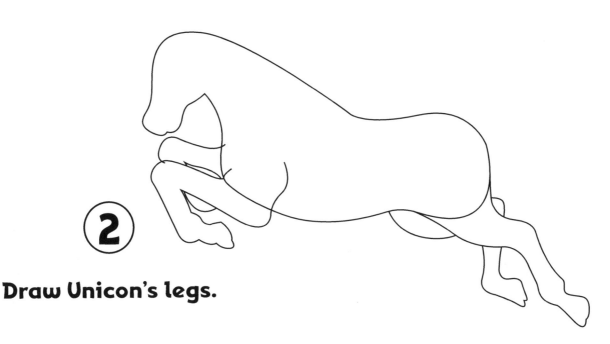

2

Draw Unicon's legs.

UNICORN 7

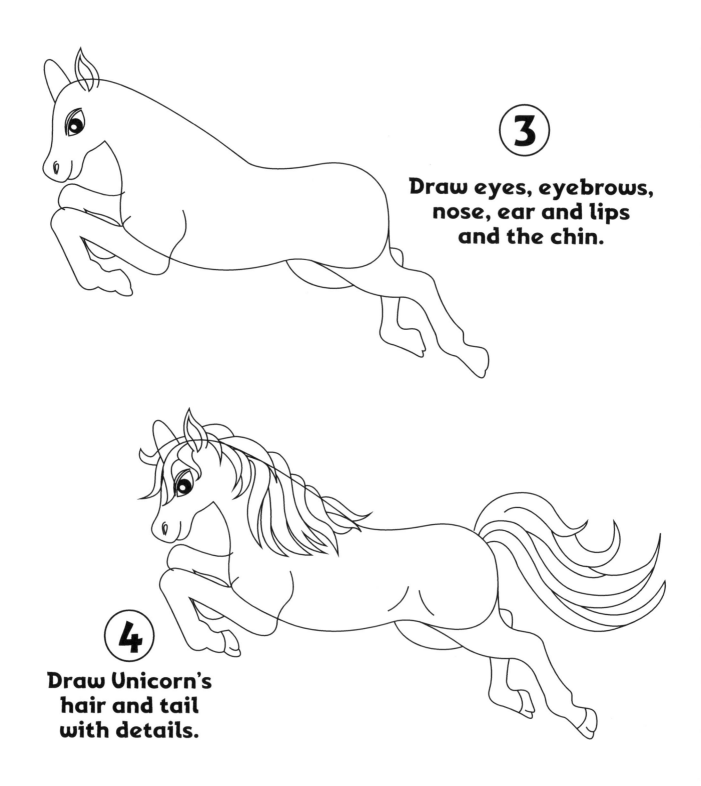

3 Draw eyes, eyebrows, nose, ear and lips and the chin.

4 Draw Unicorn's hair and tail with details.

UNICORN 7

⑤ Draw the Horn of the Unicorn.

⑥ Finally, delete all unnecessary lines to merge the body.

UNICORN 8

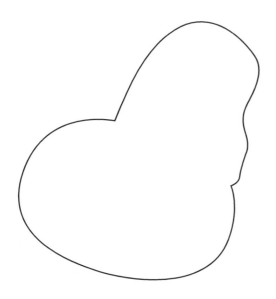

①

Draw the shape of
the Unicorn.

②

Draw Unicon's legs
lines for the belly.

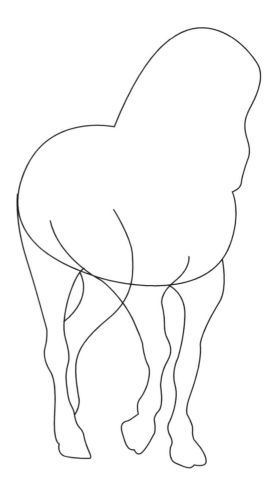

UNICORN 8

 3

Draw eyes, eyebrows, nose, ear and lips and the chin.

4

Draw Unicorn's hair and tail with details.

UNICORN 8

5 Draw the Horn of the Unicorn.

6 Finally, delete all unnecessary lines to merge the body.

UNICORN 9

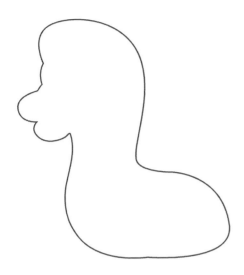

1

Draw the shape of the Unicorn.

2

Draw Unicon's legs lines for the belly.

UNICORN 9

3

Draw eyes, eyebrows, nose, ear and lips and the chin.

4

Draw Unicorn's hair and tail with details.

UNICORN 9

⑤

**Draw the Horn
of the Unicorn.**

⑥

**Finally, delete all
unnecessary lines
to merge the body.**

UNICORN 10

Draw the shape of the Unicorn.

2

Draw Unicon's legs.

UNICORN 10

3 Draw eyes, eyebrows, nose, ear and lips and the chin.

4 Draw Unicorn's hair and tail with details.

UNICORN 10

5 Draw the Horn of the Unicorn.

6 Finally, delete all unnecessary lines to merge the body.

Made in the USA
Monee, IL
02 December 2019